LOCUS

LOCUS

LOCUS

LOCUS

Smile, please

Taiwan Experience

by Sayling Wen

& Tsai Chih-chung

The 1950s : a hard time to start from scratch

The 1960s : export-oriented industries emerged and grew

The 1970s : expansion of small and medium-sized enterprises

The 1980s : full industrialization with continuous efforts

The 1990s : the new rich create a wealth of knowledge

As Taiwan steps into a new epoch, the years of 2000, 2001, 2002, 2003...appear in an ever closer perspective.

We salute to the development and growth Taiwan has undergone during the past five decades and hereby record the Taiwan Experience.

Knowledge is Power

by Li Kuo-ting （李國鼎）, Ph.D.,
Senior Advisor to the President

"Taiwan Experience" is the third book, following "Success with Money and Joy" and "Prospect", written by Sayling Wen (溫世仁). As an entrepreneur personally involved in the development of Taiwan's economy, Wen is keen in observation, prudent in thinking and has a wide-open mind toward what he saw and experienced.

The book depicts in detail the Taiwan experience of the past five decades - including the agricultural civilization in the 1950s, the industrial civilization during the period from 1960s through the '80s, and the information civilization since 1990. The development of Taiwan's economy is analyzed from four structural aspects: wealth-creating system, social system, political system and ideological system. The book serves as a witness of history and also sketches out a blueprint of future development. Readers will sense the down-to-earth attitude of an entrepreneur and the wide perspective of

an intellectual reflected in this work. "Taiwan Experience" can also be highly praised for its lucid writing, vivid examples, clear logic and simple but to-the-point content.

The achievement of Taiwan's economy has been based on the hard toil and joint efforts of all the people living on the island. Looking backward, we worked hard and took pains to build up a sound foundation for our economic development. Efforts in innovation have brought us today wealth and affluence. Small and medium-sized enterprises have become the engine of our economy. Some have transformed themselves into large corporations. Taiwanese companies have been holding a competitive advantage of great flexibility and efficiency in terms of both production and marketing. The future for us is blessed with challenges and opportunities.

As a member of governmental economic construction projects, I have been involved in many decision-making processes. I read Wen's book with great interest and feel pleased to recommend it. A famous saying reminds us that: "knowledge is power." I hope those who read this book will obtain knowledge to help further enhance Taiwan's competitiveness and create new heights of

Taiwan Experience

Taiwan Experience.

Taiwan Can Do It!

By Mr. Wu Jung-yi （吳榮義）, Ph.D.,
President of Taiwan Institute of Economic Research

The development of Taiwan's economy is often described as a "miracle". If miracle is interpreted as the achievement of something that other countries cannot achieve, then Taiwan experience is indeed a miracle. Take as an example of Taiwan's economic development, we can see that the continuous growth of an economy is closely related to the transformation of local infrastructure from a long-term perspective. The agricultural economy established by the Japanese during the colonial period built up the foundation for further development.

Then the industrial sector developed with incredible speed after WWII. The industry sector accounted for 21.3% of Taiwan's overall economic activity in the 1950s and quickly reached a record height of 47.1% in 1986. In 1996, the agricultural, industrial and service

sectors accounted for 3.3%, 35.6% and 61.1% of GDP, respectively. In fact, today's Taiwan is regarded as a service-oriented country.

As the domestic market is very limited, the growth of Taiwan's industry depends heavily on export expansion. The strong competitiveness of Taiwan-made industrial products in the international market has made our industry develop and our exports grow. From the Taiwan experience, we may conclude that export expansion, rapid industrialization and economic development are actually integrated with one another.

Taiwan's export industry is essentially carried out by small- and medium-sized enterprises (SMEs). The way that these SMEs started their business and explored international markets has played an important role in determining Taiwan's rapid economic development. The author Sayling Wen himself is a typical representative of Taiwan's successful SME story. The process of how he started his own business and strove for success is indeed a mirror of the Taiwan experience. His experience helps us understand the toil and sacrifice the SMEs had to deal with in starting up their businesses. However, the hardships the SMEs underwent in the past 50 years are often forgotten when people talk about the economic miracle of Taiwan today.

The Taiwan Institute of Economic Research (TIER) has been following closely the development of the domestic economy. Our research has focused on economic development, relevant policies and current economic conditions. Special attention is also given to the rapid changes in Taiwan's infrastructure over the past decade, future strategy and prospects. According to TIER's research, factors such as the sharp appreciation of the New Taiwan Dollar and increasing wages have eroded Taiwan's international competitiveness. Many labor-intensive manufacturing activities have had to move off-shore and therefore left a gap in local industry. Fortunately, the fast development of the machinery and electronic industries appeared on the screen and have played an important role in keeping Taiwan's exports continuously growing. The

continued success of the machinery and electronic industries is, of course, our major concern.

The main product of Wen's company, Inventec Corp. (英業達), is the portable computer. Inventec's turnover rose significantly from NT$4.7 billion in 1991 to NT$43.5 billion in 1996 when most companies suffered from a general economy slump. Their outstanding performance is truly impressive. TIER had the honor of inviting Sayling Wen to give a speech on his business experience and philosophy. Colleagues in our institute certainly benefitted a lot through Wen's speech.

I am glad to know that Sayling Wen is prepared to publish his speeches. This will benefit a wider range of readers. Wen is gifted with keen observation and has abundant business experience. He writes with clarity and ease of understanding. Readers not only share Wen's valuable experience but also discover the real Taiwan experience. It is with great pleasure that I have undertaken to write the preface and highly recommend this book.

50 Years of Taiwan Experience From the Perspective of An Entrepreneur

by Sayling Wen, Author

Once at a breakfast meeting, Prof. Dr. Alvin Toffler offered me the original English-version of his work, The Third Wave. I told him on the spot: "I have seen what you called the third wave civilization." He then asked me if I had already read the Chinese-version of The Third Wave. I replied that I had read the book and, furthermore, I had seen with my own eyes the so-called "the third wave civilization" take place in Taiwan.

Looking back on the past five decades in Taiwan, most people will agree that it has been a period full of changes and ever increasing complexity. To analyze the past fifty years from the viewpoint of the evolution of a civilization. Taiwan actually experienced all three waves of the civilization mentioned by Toffler. That are as follows:

The First Wave: Agricultural Civilization (the 1950s)

Taiwan was pragmatically in an age of agriculture in the 1950s.

The Second Wave: Industrial Civilization (the 1960s, 1970s and 1980s)
In the period from the 1960s to the 1980s, Taiwan underwent a transformation from an agricultural economy to an industrial one, thereby experiencing the second-wave civilization - industrial civilization. Industrialization reached its peak in the 1980s when Taiwan began moving toward an information age.

The Third Wave: Information Civilization (since the 1980s)
Since the 1980s, Taiwan has been turning into the third-wave civilization - information civilization in which the economic lifeblood of the society is centered on information.

Both Tsai Chih-chung (蔡志忠) and I were born in 1948 and have lived through the first fifty years of our lives. We have been there and have actually observed and been involved in Taiwan's development over the past five decades. Our hope is to write a book that serves to introduce Taiwan's experience in a simple yet thorough way. It will only take

readers two or three hours to read this book and be able to understand the phenomenon of Taiwan's economic development and phenomenon over the past fifty years. No economic theories nor exact statistical figures will be found in the book, yet a portrait of real life emerges and it tells real stories.

Lack of resources and political status notwithstanding, Taiwan with her limited size nevertheless rose up from poverty to become an economic success that is the envy of the world. How did this come about? What price did Taiwan pay for her achievement? Where will Taiwan go and how will she get there? These are the issues the book will address.

History is a mirror of time. Though it might be an oversimplified way to analyze history, this approach will nevertheless help readers easily see the complete picture.

Time has been used as a vertical axle and the structure of civilization as a horizontal axle to analyze Taiwan's economic development over the past five decades. The analysis has been done decade by decade. Each decade represents a unit for further investigation reflecting the changes in the wealth-creating system which led to changes in the social and political systems and in the way people think. We did not put "Mr." before the names of important persons to avoid a lengthy description. For people living on the island and sharing a common life, it is more natural to call people simply by name.

I was just a kid in the 1950s. In the 1960s I was a student in high school and then at the university. Descriptions about these two decades were mainly based on my memories and readings. To get more information, I had an interview with the senior advisor to the President, Dr. Li Kuo-ting for his advice. Dr. Li at the age of 88 deliberated for two hours on the economic history of Taiwan. When he talked, it seemed that he was back in the good old days - when he was a hero in helping to create Taiwan's miracle. It has been my great honor that Senior Advisor Li Kuo-ting and President Wu Jong-yi of the Taiwan Institute of Economic Research wrote the prefaces to this book.

The last section provides some predictions and prospects. As time proceeds apace and brings changes with it, our predictions of the future might have to be amended. In the belief that readers have their own perspective on what they

read, we have chosen to use a positive tone and have avoided using words such as "possible", "probably", etc.

Suffering fosters growth. In the past five decades, the Chinese with diligence, intelligence and perseverance have created an economic miracle on Taiwan. The fifty years were not easy ones. As we now reap the fruits of economic achievement and look forward to a promising future, let us give thanks to those who have sown the fertile Taiwanese soil with their tears and blood over the past five decades.

Note: The Third Wave, published in 1980, is the second book of futurist Alvin Toffler. The book uses technology as twin axles to describe the revolutionary changes in new technologies and in a technology-driven society. The author regards the agrarian revolution that have taken place 10,000 years ago as the first wave of civilization. The second wave was the industrial revolution. The technological and social changes that have occurred since the mid-1950 are regarded as the third wave, a new civilization also referred to as the post-industrial civilization. The book points out that future new industries will be based on computer, electronic, information and biochemical technologies. It also predicts the popularity of flexible or small-run production, niche market and moonlighting jobs. The new trend toward a demassified media is also predicted. There is a new type of system in which production combines with marketing and sales and by means of which producers become consumers. Under the new system, the work place will move from the factory back to the home. The book also provides a new portrait of society in which political and national regimes are reconstructed in many ways.

The first wave of civilization: the agrarian age

The second wave of civilization: the industrial age

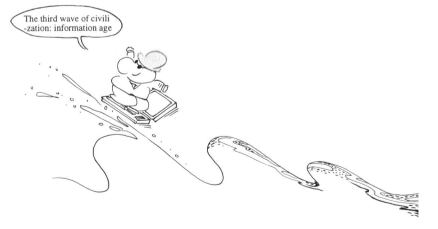

The third wave of civili -zation: information age

Taiwan Experience

Contents

Knowledge is Power／by Li Kuo-ting（李國鼎）

Taiwan Can Do It!／by Mr. Wu Jung-yi （吳榮義）

50 Years of Taiwan Experience - From the Perspective of An Entrepreneur／by Sayling Wen, Author（溫世仁）

Chapter *1*

Hard Time——Born into Poverty and Suffering（*p.21*）
1．The 1950s
2．Waves of Civilization

Chapter *2*

The Emergence of Export-Oriented Industries ——Ringing the Bell of Hope（*p.33*）
3．The 1960s
4．Social Movement in the 1960s
5．The Political Situation in the 1960s.

Chapter **3**

The Growth of SMEs - The Bloom of Beautiful Flowers（*p.47*）

6 . The 1970s.

7 . Social Waves of the 1970s

8 . Political Waves of the 1970s

Chapter **4**

Full Industrialization——Taiwan is Drowning in Money!（*p.67*）

9 . The 1980s

10 . Social Waves of the 1980s

11 . Political Waves of the 1980s

12 . Waves of Thought of the 1980s

Chapter **5**

New Wealth-Creating System ——Creating a Wealth Through Knowledge（*p.91*）

13 . The 1990s

14 . Social Waves of the 1990s

15 . Political Waves of the 1990s

16 . Waves of Thought in the 1990s

17 . Looking Back on the Past 50 years

Taiwan Experience

Chapter *6*

Future Days ——Let Ideals Bloom in Year 2000 （*p.117*）
18 . Creating a New Future

Chapter *7*

Give Thanks to Everyone（*p.121*）

A Cartoonist's Taiwan Experience/Tsai Chi-Chung（*p.123*）

Chapter **1**

Hard Time——Born into Poverty and Suffering

The ocean cannot be made at once, you have to start from a stream.
——Anonymous

The multi-purpose wooden bench of the 1950s

It was usually a long wooden bench.

Sometimes it was used as our dinner table.

In the evening it was a desk for kids.

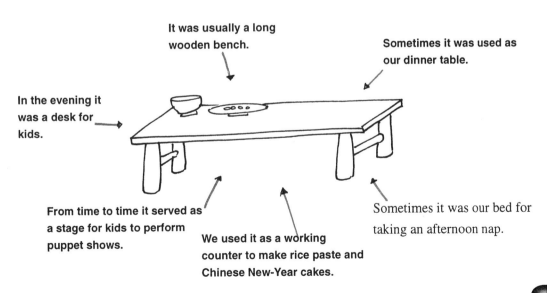

From time to time it served as a stage for kids to perform puppet shows.

We used it as a working counter to make rice paste and Chinese New-Year cakes.

Sometimes it was our bed for taking an afternoon nap.

1.The 1950s

Striving in Poverty and Improving by Continuous Revolutions

I was just a kid in the 1950s, the so-called decade of hard times. How bitter those days were can be reflected by a few figures. Most entrepreneurs typically have no clear idea of what those statistics represent, and are plagued by all the statistics often quoted by economists. However, for all entrepreneurs and myself, we are very concerned about four basic figures: wages, per capita national income, export value and foreign exchange reserves.

1. Wages: the amount paid as wages directly reflected our competitiveness and cost.
2. Per capita national income: gross national production figures divided by the figure of the total population.
3. Export value: the total value materialized by export industries.
4. Foreign exchange reserves: the figure obtained by deducting outgoing foreign currency from incoming foreign currency.

These figures in the 1950s do not make much sense as the exchange rate of the New Taiwan Dollar against the US green back fluctuated. We can only take the figures as a rough estimate. It was reported that in the '50s the per capita national income was below US$50, some other reports indicated that it was below US$80. We can get a rough idea by the following figures:

Monthly wage: US$0.00
Per capita national income: below US$80
Export value: US$100 million
Foreign exchange reserves: 0

Sisters no. 1,2,.3, 4, 5 and the little brother, let's cheer! Mom said we'll have an extra dish today..

1. Poverty

It seems that children of today do not know anything about poverty. In fact, Taiwan in the '50s was very poor. The story I want to share with you is about how a five-year-old boy living in central Taiwan in 1953 saw and experienced poverty. I was that five-year-old boy. Let me tell you how poor Taiwan used to be by describing some phenomena.

The first scenario was that we did not have a table or chairs at mealtime. At that time in a rural village, a

wooden bench was the table we used for meals. The bench served different functions: adults would lie down on the bench under a shady tree. They moved the bench over and sat on it to watch a street show, if there happened to be one. We didn't have a dining table or chairs. At mealtime, the bench was moved outside for mom to set bowls and meal plates. We used to stand up or squat on our heels while eating. There was no rice in the bowls but some sweet potato slices, somewhat similar to the French fries now available at McDonald's. We ate the sweet potatoes unpeeled. Adults would sprinkle a few grains of rice on top of the rough sweet potato slices. This was called "sweet potato pouridge." There were no vegetables nor any meat to speak of. With the "pouridge", we used to have minced fried scallion with non-processed salt granulates that were about the size of peanuts.

We didn't wear shoes to school. As a pre-schooler, I noticed that all kids went to primary school barefoot. I learned that students could get their first pair of shoes when they entered middle school. In the evening, there was no light, not to mention electricity. Adults put on oil lamps until seven or eight o'clock. Kids would have to catch some glowworms and keep them inside a bottle for illumination during dark nights. What was worse is that we didn't have toilet paper. We used a slice of bamboo to scratch away excrement. In the kitchen there was a cloth. When the cloth was pulled wide open as a screen, the kitchen became our simple shower room. This was the scenario I saw in the '50s.

2. Land Reform

Land reform was in fact completed in 1954. The Provincial Governor, Chen Cheng (陳誠) who later became Vice President, carried out the program in three planned stages: first, farm rent was reduced to a ceiling of 37.5% of total land crops; then public agrarian land was sold; and finally the "land to the tiller" program, which made tenants into land owners, was implemented. Landlords were duly compensated by stock shares of public enterprises. These measure initiated the first stage of industrialization in Taiwan. Though land reform was completed in 1954, rural life under the agrarian regime was still very poor.

3. Military Regime

Politics was dominated by the two million troops led by former President Chiang Kai-shek over six million local

inhabitants. The total population was around seven or eight million. The military control was so harsh that even we kids felt the oppressive atmosphere.

4. US Economic Aid

I still remember the US aid given to Taiwan when I was a primary school boy. A boy's idea about US aid was that we could get wheat flour from a western church and that flour sacks could be further used to make underpants. People were fond of making underpants out of flour sacks because the fabric was of good quality. It was common for us to go out wearing only such pants which showed the hand-shaking trade mark of the Sino-American Flour Plant. It took me several years to realize that US aid was very important in supporting Taiwan's economy. According to Li Kuoting, US Aid played a key role in stabilizing Taiwan's economy and implementing public construction.

5. Import Control

Imports were prohibited. It was big news if someone brought into Taiwan something from abroad. People would be very surprised and curious to see what he got from abroad. Later I learned that the measure was called "import substitution." The measure was taken to protect infant local industries and to nurture an entrepreneurial climate.

6. The Birth Control Campaign with the Slogan "333"

When I was in the fifth and sixth grades in primary school, the government started the "333" birth control campaign. What was it? This was a campaign that advocated the concept of birth control. New couples were encouraged to have their first child three years after marriage, to have a maximum of three children and to wait three years after the birth of each child. In an agrarian society, more children means volume production. It was quite senseless to promote birth control and therefore the campaign was not successful. Nevertheless, we saw some results of the campaign in the 1960s.

I graduated from primary school in 1960 when there was as yet no compulsory nine-year education system. I had to pass a joint-entrance examination to enter middle school.

The island down there is called FORMOSA and also TAIWAN. It is a beautiful island but the country is very small and poor.

2. Waves of Civilization

Analyzing Taiwan's wealth-creating system from the Perspective of Dr. Toffler's Civilization Structure Graph.

Let us take a look at Toffler's civilization structure before going on with the 1960s.

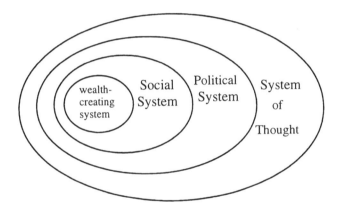

I derived my civilization structure from Dr. Toffler. According to his theory, civilization starts with a wealth-creating system. Then a social system is created along with the wealth-creating system. For example, thousands of years ago, our ancestors created a plantation method along the Yellow River. Plantation was the method of creating profit. The wealth-creating method created a rural life and rural villages based on

an agrarian economy. The villages gradually expanded outwards which eventually led to border disputes, hence a political system was created to make decisions and settle disputes. Underlying the political system, a system of beliefs comprised of heaven, earth, emperor, personal relatives and teacher began to take shape. Thus, a self-contained agrarian civilization was formed.

The following analysis of Taiwan's history in the '60s is based on the above-mentioned civilization structure.

I was a student uninvolved in any social activity in the 1960s. I finished my elementary school, spent six years in the middle school affiliated with National Normal University and four years at National Taiwan University. I researched and found out that wages at that time averaged around US$2 to 3. The exchange rate of NT$ against US$ was in a state of chaos. It was only in the 60s that the exchange rate was stabilized at NT$40 against US$1 to enhance exports. My family owned a small shop for servicing household electricity and pumps. The wages we paid a worker was about NT$80 per month. The per capita national income was around US$150 and export value reached almost US$200 million. The export amount of US$100 million in the '50s came entirely from agricultural products. In the '60s, export products had added value and Taiwan had accumulated US$76 million in foreign exchange reserves.

Monthly wage: US$2-3

Per capita national income: US$150

Export value: US$200 million

Foreign exchange reserves: US$76 million

Export-oriented industries were nurtured in the 1960s. Let us first look at the changes that took place in Taiwan's wealth-creating system.

I earn only a few hundred dollars each month. When will I ever be able to buy a home of my own?

Taiwan Experience

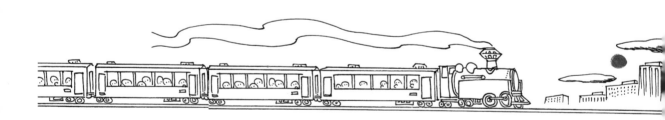

Chapter **2**

The Emergence of Export-Oriented Industries ——Ringing the Bell of Hope

Pray for miracles but don't rely on miracles.
——Jewish saying.

3. The 1960s

The Wealth-Creating System Along With Nascent Export-Oriented Industries

1. Selling Labor

I cared very much about what was happening in our society even though I was still a student. In a nutshell, Taiwan in the '60s could sell nothing but our native labor force. The Taiwanese, once ruled by the Japanese for 50 years (1895-1945), and then under the authoritarian regime of the KMT, were very diligent and docile. Furthermore, their wages were very low. The wealth-creating system therefore started with simple processing lines (small-scale production) in labor-intensive industries.

2. Incentives for Domestic and Foreign Investments

The government was committed to improving the investment environment. "The Statute for Encouragement on Investment" was promulgated to encourage the channeling of local private savings into investments and attracting foreign investment on made-for-export industries. Renowned companies such as GE and RCA started their manufacturing factories in Taiwan and created numerous job opportunities.

At the initial phase of development, we sold our native labor to attract foreign capital. But it was not good enough just to sell our labor; the government then set up several export-processing zones to create more job opportunities for the local labor force.

3. Establishing Export-Processing Zones (1966)

The government established three export-processing zones (in Chienjen Kaohsiung, Tantzi Taichung and Nantzi Kaohsiung) in years between 1966 and 1968. This was actually the best measure for expanding job opportunities. As undergraduates, we used to joke about the three zones as labor communes. However, the labor force was the only resource we had to transform Taiwan into an industrialized nation.

In terms of industrialization, we used to quote 3M: Material, Market and Money. Then Manpower was added. Again experts include Management, Machine and Method to make 7M. In the 1960s, the only M that Taiwan could provide was manpower. We had to make full use of our manpower. That is, to provide everyone with a job so that we could develop our industry and transform our society into an industrialized one.

In fact, the idea of export-processing zones was created by Taiwan and the first export-processing zone was established in Taiwan. Nowadays, many developing countries have followed suit.

4. Expansion of Private Enterprises (OEM vendors and agents of foreign firms)

Private companies gradually accumulated the needed technological and management skills learned from their foreign partners. In the past, smaller-scaled production houses served as vendors that made components for export-oriented factories. In addition to being satellite factories, these production houses also acted as export agents for their clients. Larger-scaled companies had a different approach and they obtained the agency of foreign electrical appliances for domestic sales. Limited by the import control policy, these companies imported completely knocked down (CKD) kits for assembly and re-sale in Taiwan. This was how local companies expand their business activities.

5. The Growth of the Textile Industry

As we were short of foreign currency, we had to substitute domestic products for imports. Thanks to the skills and experiences of the textile entrepreneurs who came to Taiwan with President Chiang Kai-shek, Taiwan's textile industry was well developed and

3M
MATERIAL
MARKET
MONEY

7M
MATERIAL
MARKET
MONEY
MANPOWER
MANAGEMENT
MACHINE
METHOD

No matter how many Ms are quoted, I go to McDonald's for lunch.

McDONALD'S

integrated the up-stream, middle-stream and down-stream sectors. The textile industry has had a significant influence on Taiwan's economic development, and it remained the largest export industry in the country until the 1980s.

6. The Rise of the Plastics Industry
Through governmental support, the now famous entrepreneur Wang Yung-ching（王永慶）received a US Loan to expand his business from a polyethylene (PE) plant with a daily production of 4 tons into a multinational giant that presently owns several plants at home and abroad. He also established several plastics processing factories to ensure outlets for the plastic raw materials produced by his factories. With his perseverance and his persistent personality, Wang Yung-ching has established the largest plastics kingdom in the world. He has also earned the title of "Master of Management" in Taiwan.

Let us look at what happened in our society during this same period. According to Toffler's theory, "the social system changes in accordance with the changes of the wealth-creating system."

4. Social Movement in the 1960s

The Social Changes with the Budding Export-Oriented Industries

1. A woman worker's wish

This is the title of a pop song at that time. The song was about the heartstrings of a rural girl working in a city factory. The song was very popular because it reflected the mobility of a nascent industrial society. Population in an agrarian society used to be scattered here and there. In an industrial society, population becomes concentrated in places where factories are located. Taipei, Kaohsiung and Taichung are the three cities that benefited by a heavy concentration of factories.

2. Window-seeing TV viewers

People of my age probably still remember the year 1962 when Taiwan Television (TTV) launched the first broadcast in Taiwan. The price of a black-and-white television set at that time was around NT$5,000. Only a very few families could afford such a luxury. Everyday after school, children like me from poor families would hurry to occupy a space outside the window of a house equipped with a TV. In order to have a good view, we kept standing outside and restrained ourselves from taking a leak lest our good position be occupied by someone else. Since then our lives became richer in terms of entertainment. One characteristic of an industrial society is that most people had the same entertainment -- watching the same program at the same time. Subconsciously, I sensed the distance between the rich and the poor.

3. Population Policy : "333" Birth Control Measure

The slogan made to carry out the birth control measure changed from "333" to "2 is ideal".[1] The idea of birth control was resisted by members of the agrarian society that preferred many children for labor. In the industrial society, the smaller the family size, the easier

for people to move on to better jobs. Thanks to Chiang Mon-lin (蔣夢麟), the Chairman of Agricultural Restoration Council (農復會) and Hsu Shih-chu (許世鉅), the birth control concept was actively introduced and promoted in rural villages. It was furthered advocated by Li Kuo-ting in urban areas and by Hsieh Tung-ming (謝東閔) in other areas throughout Taiwan. The "2 is ideal" birth control measure became a national campaign and was gradually accepted by the general public. However, the presumption for most Chinese was that at least one of the two children must be male. It is ideal to have two boys and it is ideal as well to have one boy and one girl. However, if a family has two girls, the parents would continue to have children. In that case, it was quite common to see families with four or five girls and the youngest a boy. According to the statistics compiled by sociologist Tsai Song-ling (柴松林), females born in the '60s and '70s far outnumbered males in the same period. That is the main reason why there are so many more eligible females than eligible males today.

*Note 1: The "2 is ideal" slogan advocated the concept of having two children in each family.

5. The Political Situation in the 1960s.

Political Changes That Came With the Nascent Export-Oriented Industries.

The role of the political system under a budding export-oriented economy.

1. Foreign Trade Policy (exchange rate of NT$ against US$ set at 40:1, tax rebates on exports, low-interest loan)

The political environment remained unchanged, which contributed to the establishment of an export-promotion environment. Yin Chung-jung （尹仲容） made a remarkable adjustment of the export exchange rate in 1958 and eventually stabilized the exchange value of NT$ against US$ at 40:1 in 1960. In addition, the US Economic Aid Council (美援會) together with other competent authorities drafted the "Statute for Encouragement on Investment" to promote made-for-export industries. The government also rebated the import tariff and commodity tax levied on raw materials, parts and components imported for domestic processing and re-export. In the meantime, the traditional concept of land for agricultural purposes was changed. It was encouraged to appropriate

farmland for industrial purposes. All these efforts were made to build up a favorable climate for the export industry.

2. The End of US Economic Aid and the Involvement of the US in the Vietnam War

The US Aid ended in 1965. In fact, the Aid was called off when the central government moved from the mainland to Taiwan. The US resumed the Aid to Taiwan in 1950 when the Korean War erupted. The US Aid which accounted for 10% of our GDP ended in 1965 when the US became involved in the Vietnam War. Generally speaking, the end of the US Aid did not have any impact on us as our export promotion economy was by that time smoothly underway.

3. The Contribution of Yen Chia-kan (嚴家淦) to the Country's Economic Development

During the 30 years from 1950 to 1980, Yen Chia-kan was committed to the country's economic development. At the post of Minister of Finance, he established the budget system to regulate the yet unstable economy. He fully supported the three phases for carrying out land reform and discretely privatized four public enterprises by the "land to the tillers" statute. Based on this statute, land owners were compensated with shares of public enterprises and became private entrepreneurs. Yen Chia-kan and Yin Chung-jung gave the initial impetus to the establishment of the private sector. In 1958 he resumed the post of Minister of Finance and carried out tax reform to balance government budgets.

Realizing the importance of economic development to the country, he supported the "Statute for Encouragement on Investment" proposed by the US Economic Aid Council. The Statute encouraged investment in export-oriented industries by giving investors tax reductions as one of the main incentives. Thanks to Yen's convincing analysis and presentation to the nation's legislators, the Statute was quickly approved and passed in the Legislative Yuan.

Yen showed his political sauvy by appointing Chiang Ching-kuo（蔣經國） to be Minister of Defense, Li Kuo-ting Minister of Economic Affairs and Yen Cheng-hsin（閻振興） Minister of Education in 1965 when the cabinet was reshuffled.

In 1969 when the cabinet was partially reshuffled, he proposed that President Chiang Kai-shek appoint Chiang Ching-kuo as Vice Premier and in the meantime Chairman of the Economic Cooperation Council. In 1973 when the cabinet was again reshuffled, Yen concentrated on the post of Vice President and left the post of Premier to Chiang Ching-kuo.

In 1975 when President Chiang Kai-shek passed away, Yen succeeded to the presidency until 1978 when Chiang Ching-kuo was elected as President. That same year Yen Chia-kan retired. We can see that Yen's contribution to the country was remarkable and that Chiang Ching-kuo did not obtain the country's leadership overnight; instead, he arrived at his position step-by-step over the course of more than 10 years.

Chiang Kai-shek's secrets

4. The Leadership of Chiang Ching-kuo (a leader with power, experience and wisdom)

Vice President Chen Cheng passed away in 1965 when Chiang Ching-kuo was the Minister of Defense. Under a political regime dominated by totalitatarian rule, the number-two man's decease had a significant impact on the evolution of Chiang Ching-kuo, the son of Chiang Kai-shek. Later the junior Chiang became the country's leader, embodying power, experience and wisdom. His leadership was critical to Taiwan's economic development.

5. Leadership by the Two Chiangs and Experienced Technocrats

An adhoc committee was formed to promote industrialization in Taiwan under the two Chiang's leadership and by a team of unselfish government technocrats. Their efforts made an indispensable contribution to Taiwan's economic development in the following 25 years.

6. To Recover Mainland China vs. To Study Abroad

In schools teachers taught us about the task of recovering Mainland China. Students, however, only cared about advanced study in the US. While studying in the middle school of National Normal University, I had many classmates who had already started preparing for future study in America. At the university, everyone pretended that he would go abroad for study. Otherwise, no girl would date a guy with no plans to

study in America.

7. The Cultural Revolution in Mainland China (1966 - 1976)
In the meantime, the Cultural Revolution occurred in China. That was a disaster to China but a good opportunity for the four Asian Little Dragons (ASIA NIES countries) to strengthen their economies.

We have reviewed changes in the wealth-creating system, social system, political system and the system of thoughts of the '60s. Let us continue to look at the decade of the 1970s with which I am more familiar. I graduated from National Taiwan University (NTU) in 1970 and left the army service in 1971. I started to get involved in business affairs. Then I entered graduate school and at the same time, I took on a part-time job to earn some money.

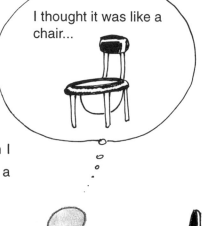

I thought it was like a chair...

National Taiwan University (NTU) built a new library in 1970 when I was about to graduate from the school. I visited the library for the main purpose of seeing the lavatory inside the building. I was very curious as I had never seen a flush toilet with a seat. That was the first time I saw a flush toilet with a seat in my life.

Chapter **3**

The Growth of SMEs——The Bloom of Beautiful Flowers

To see the garden is to know the gardener.

——Anonymous

6.The 1970s

The Textile and Plastics Industries Paved the Road for Petrochemical Industry

In 1970 the average monthly wage for a blue-collar worker was NT$400 and the per capita national income was around US$400. In the aftermath of the foreign trade reform conducted in the 60s, the value of exports amounted to US$2 billion. In 1975, we had accumulated US$1 billion in foreign exchange reserves.

Monthly wage: US$10
Per capita national income: US$400
Export value: US$2 billion
Foreign exchange reserves: US$1 billion (1975)

As Taiwan had accumulated some capital, the SMEs started taking off.

How did the SMEs grow and expand? The vendors and agents of foreign companies gradually accumulated their own wealth, experience and talents. Then they made their own products for sale. Recently, I made a speech in Malaysia. On that occasion someone asked me: "We know that you Taiwanese are very hard-working and therefore you enjoy a booming economy. But how did you sell what you made?" That was a good question.

1. Fat-hen-style Peddlers

The way we started selling products was like the way fat
hens run around everywhere. We brought with us
samples and catalogues to the airport. Every time we
saw a foreigner coming out of customs, we would rush
forward to ask him or her to buy something. We also
waited in the lobbies of different hotels. As long as we
saw a foreigner, we immediately approached him or her
as a potential customer. At that time actually not many
businessmen came to Taiwan. I remember once I
approached a foreigner who turned out to be a teacher.
He was very confused and couldn't understand why I
kept trying to sell products to him. Well, that was how we
started to sell our products. Then came with the
marketing channels of IPO and OEM.

2. IPO and OEM

As more and more products were being manufactured in
Taiwan, some American and Japanese companies set
up their international purchasing offices (IPOs) in
Taiwan. We would always take samples and quotations

with us when visiting these IPOs. The local employees of the IPOs then would select some products and display them in their show windows. (How lucky the slected were!) These products on display would have the chance of being sold to foreign buyers. When foreign buyers did come to visit the IPOs, we lined up and stood outside their offices. The IPOs would never offer us any chair. The buyer would sit inside comfortably and point out whom he wanted to meet. The way in which the buyer selected from among Taiwanese firms was similar to the way in which an emperor would select a concubine. The selected seller would then hurry inside to introduce his or her products. This is the scenario of how the SMEs sold their products.

Some enterprises gradually expanded and started to accept OEM (Original Equipment Manufacturing) orders. In this case, the order-receiving enterprise manufactured products according to the drawings or samples provided by the foreign buyer. The cost of raw materials and the profit to be earned were clearly discussed and listed between the two parties. Then business started.

3. The Calculator Industry (the birth of ODM concept)
The 1970s gave rise to the calculator industry which was very important to Taiwan's future industrial development. At that time

most entrepreneurs in Taiwan started their businesses from scratch and by labor work. The calculator industry was the only industry that involved well-educated university graduates. It was an innovative industry with a rosy future. The industry used local talent to create and design products. Therefore, local companies were able to make their own products and sell them to their OEM customers. That was the origin of the ODM (Original Design Manufacturing) concept.

** The Calculator Industry of Taiwan

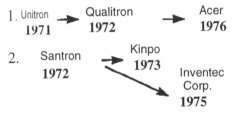

Many people thought that Barry Lam (林百里) and I were the first to make electronic calculators. This is in fact not the case. The development of the calculator industry started with an IC packaging company called Unitron (環宇) in Hsin Chu. Unitron developed its first calculator in 1971. The same year when the calculator was further simplified to one single IC, my classmate Barry Lam and I also developed a calculator in the laboratory. Together with San Ter Co. (三德) which originally made

asbestos, we set up a new company called Santron Electronics (三愛) to make electronic calculators. Our company was one of the first manufacturers in the early phase of the calculator industry. You might wonder why Unitron has been forgotten by people. Well, the company had some problems with product quality and then the company closed down calculators business. Afterwards, a man called Lin Sen (林森) with a background in textiles saved up enough capital to establish Qualitron (榮泰). He recruited all the engineers that had originally worked in Unitron. The chief engineer of Unitron was Stan Shih (施振榮) , who later became the leader in the information industry.

During the same period, Teco (東元) , the big manufacturer of motors and household electrical appliances, also mass-produced calculators. Their production of calculators was halted, however, due to a shortage of young engineers.

Before the establishment of Qualitron, Santron was the only manufacturer of calculators. Santron started with a capital investment of NT$2,500,000. We did not have any capital as we were employed and paid by San Ter for our technical expertise and through Bonus. Twelve of us, all students of National Taiwan University (NTU) , started our own production line in June in a corner of the dormitory of San Ter. In October of that year, our employer visited us during his routine inspection tour in San Ter. He asked how much our products were and found out that a few cartons of our products were worth much more than the total output of his factory that occupied a space of 33,050 square meters. Realizing the great potential of the electronics industry, we invested NT$2,500,000 to establish Santron and earned NT$10 million the very first year.

Then six of the twelve National Taiwan University (NTU) partners left Santron to establish Kinpo (金寶) with Hsu Chao-Ying （許潮英）, an entrepreneur in Taoyuan. The competition that began between Unitron and Santron then switched to Oualitron and Kinpo. For the first two and three years, Qualitron took a commanding position against other competitors while Kinpo grew at a stable pace. In 1975 Yeh, Kuo-I (葉國一) and Robert Cheng (鄭清和) left Santron to establish Inventec (英業達). Since then, Santron switched its main production line to stereos and gradually suspended its calculator line. Qualitron,

Just follow the book.

Can you really assemble them?

meanwhile, was maintaining its leading position in calculator production. However, Qualitron was a conglomerate and was hurt financially by the poor operation of its other companies and was forced to close down in 1976. Stan Shih recruited Qualitron's engineers and established Acer the same year. He did not have much available capital. With his partners he collected a capital of NT$1 million and rented an apartment in Ming-Sheng East Road of Taipei to produce microprocessors.

Kinpo, much stronger than before, purchased the factory and facilities originally belonging to Qualitron. In 1979 as General Manager of Kinpo, I frequently paid visit to Acer after dinner. Acer was located very close to Kinpo. Though small in size, Acer was able to recruit many talented young men with high morality. In Acer even the seats next to the lavatory were taken by graduates from NTU! My company was not able to recruit even a single graduate form NTU. Acer was engaged in a new production industry and Stan Shih himself had a special charm over young people. By 1979 he almost ran out of his NT$1 million investment whereas Kinpo enjoyed NT$100 million in profits

Welcome home-coming scholars

←

Hsin-chu Science-Based Industrial Park

before taxes. The outcome of the competition between the two companies was clear. In the meantime, Inventec ranked as the second largest producer of calculators. Even now the combined outputs of Kinpo and Inventec together still accounts for 40% of world calculator production. To develop and expand, the two companies moved their manufacturing bases abroad to Thailand, Malaysia and China.

According to my personal experience, the calculator industry in the '70s marked an important turning point in that it attracted well-educated persons to take part in Taiwan's industrial development. Today the calculator is no longer a major industrial product. Acer's defeat in the battle of the calculator business, however, turned out to be a blessing in disguise. Stan Shih with his vital leadership conducted the information industry into a new era.

4. Industrial Technology Research Institute (ITRI工研院) Established in 1973
Electronic Research & Service Organization (ERSO電子所) Established in 1974
IC Model Factories established in years 1975 - 1979

Let me show you all kinds of product from my company.Are you interested?

Institute for Information Industry (III資策會) established
With the support of Li Kuo-ting, Fan Hsien-chi（方齊
賢）, the president of ITRI, recruited from America
many outstanding experts who had graduated from
NTU and earned their Ph.D. in the US. These people
included Hu Ting-hwa（胡定華）、Shih Chin-tay（史欽
泰）、Yang Ting-yuan（楊丁元）and Chung Ching-chu
（章青駒）. They were invited back to their home
country to develop the IC industry. Robert Tsao（曹興
誠）who had been working in Taiwan also jointed the
IC ad hoc. He was the vice president of ERSO during
the period when Hu Ting-hwa served as ERSO's
president.

After Fan Chi-hsien retired from ITRI, Morris Chung（
張忠謀）, a senior expert in the IC industry, came back
from America to succeed as president of ITRI.

Taiwan's IC production technology was first introduced
by RCA whose technology at that time was not too
advanced. Therefore, even people in the industry were
not optimistic about the IC industry in Taiwan.
However, the infant industry in the '70s became the
country's most important industry by late '80s. Today

the IC industry is the most capital-rich and well-staffed industry in Taiwan with great deal of potential. People naturally tend to criticize the government for inefficiency. However, I am sure that the government has been highly efficient in implementing the IC industry. Otherwise, the IC industry today in Taiwan would be very weak.

5. Establishment of Hsin-chu Science-Based Industrial Park

At the end of 1979 the government established Hsin-chu Science-Based Industrial Park to attract "brains" from the US. If the export processing zones of the '60s were called labor communes, the science-based park became a brain commune.

Let us see what happened to society in the era of SMEs.

7.Social Waves of the 1970s

Social Changes Along With the Growth of SMEs

1. Turn your living room into a factory

"Turn your living room into a factory " was the most famous saying by Shieh Tung-ming （謝東閔）, then the Provincial Governor and later the Vice President. He emphasized: "Don't cry about not having a production factory. The living room can be your factory." He advocated the idea and people followed suit. Therefore, household living rooms served as premises to earn foreign currency. They were the factories for producing plastic flowers, Christmas trees and so on. As a river is made by drops of water, so is affluence accumulated by small amounts of income. However, there was a price to pay for what we earned. For example, the living room for Chinese children originally was a place to learn how to behave well. Since the premise was taken over for production purpose, children were not properly educated and some of them turned into the black sheep of society. This has made a negative impact on the social environment.

2. Laurels and humiliations

I would like to emphasize how difficult it was for the SMEs to get orders in the '70s remember that I once visited an electronics trade fair in the US. In fact, and most Taiwanese merchants I were not qualified to exhibit at the fair. We could only stand outside an exhibition booth and demonstrate our product samples to the exhibitors. They bought something if they liked the samples, otherwise they would just shout us away. Most Taiwanese companies brought with them packs of samples in different sizes. We lined up and waited to meet our potential clients. I remember a scene in which that a merchant in front of me was showing his digital clock in display tubes to a buyer. The buyer threw the sample on the ground. Moreover, he broke all the tubes with his shoe while cursing him "son-of-bitch". The Taiwanese merchant was so embarrassed and did not know what to do. Such misery was the common fate of most Taiwanese merchants. Companies in the electronic business were luckier when compared with those in the sundry business. The latter had to exhaust themselves by taking foreign buyers to fool around in night clubs.

It was difficult to materialize sales, but it was even

more painful to meet deadlines in production. Most companies worked on a twenty-four schedule.

My company had a vendor that made name plates. One night the owner of the vendor, exhausted by long-term overtime work, accidentally cut off one of his fingers. He was rushed to the emergency room of a hospital. When informed of the misfortune by the purchasing department, I became very worried and asked a member of my purchasing staff to see him in the hospital. By the time he arrived at the hospital, the owner of the vendor was already back at his factory. The staff member went to the factory. He saw how the owner of the vendor with one hand hung in a bandage, pulled open machine, took out his cut-off finger and mashed flesh. He used his unhurt hand to wash off the cut-off finger with a spraying gun.

He assured my staff member that he would make the product delivery next morning as originally scheduled. My staff phoned me and said:"Mr. President, the vendor left the hospital. He finished his work in his factory. He assured me that the delivery for tomorrow morning will be made....." After listening to him, I lost my temper and couldn't help but shout, "My goodness! The delivery is not what concerns me!" Having hung up the phone, I burned with complex emotions within me. Over the years, our fellow people have suffered and sacrificed a lot in exchange for the economic success; I wondered how much longer such a scenario would last? How much more would we need to pay?

Our SMEs survived in a very difficult situation. While we wear the laurels of the Taiwan experience and show off our economic miracle, we should not forget that the glory was obtained by those small-potato individuals who turned their living rooms into factories and made sales on the streets. Today's glory was earned by their blood, sweat and tears and even their humiliation.

3. A house sold for NT$10,000 per ping (3.305 m^2 or 35.58 ft^2)
The big news in the '70s was that some people sold their houses at price NT$10,000 per ping. That was an incredible news as houses were usually available only a few thousands per ping .

4. Department stores, dim-sum restaurants and night

clubs

Department stores, Cantonese dim-sum restaurants and night clubs were now fashionable places to go to.

5. Small enterprises earned foreign currency but big enterprises made profits selling to the local population

At the end of the '70s, most SMEs had more than 50% of their products made for export. It was said that small enterprises earned US$ but big enterprises earned NT$. The big enterprises were those engaged in insurance, real-estate and development. This situation lasted until the '90s .

8.Political Waves of the 1970s

The Political System and Thinking during the Period When the SMEs Began to Take Off

There were several major events that had a significant impact on Taiwan:

1. Taiwan's withdrawal from the United Nations (1971)

2. Taiwan's severing of diplomatic ties with Japan (1972)

3. The first oil crisis (1973)

4. The launching of the Ten Major Development Projects

The Ten Major Development Projects was a turning point for Taiwan's economy. Included in the program were grand construction projects such as the North-South Highway, the Taoyuan CKS International Airport, a major steel mill and ship-building plant. The Projects provided a suitable living environment for the people of Taiwan and a solid basis for the enterprises to expand.

5. The passing of President Chiang Kai-shek (1975)

6. The age of Chiang Ching-kuo (1975-1988)

He was a sauvy leader rich in political experience. With his unselfish and outstanding staff which included Lee

Teng-hui (the current President), Lin Yang-kang, Sun Yun-hsiuan and Li Kuo-ting, he helped build a fully-industrialized country in a period of 25 years.

7. The passing of Chou En-lai and Mao Tse-tung (1976)

8. The Formosa Magazine Incident in Kaohsiung (1976)

9. Taiwan's severing of diplomatic ties with the USA (1979)

Despite the diplomatic setbacks of the 1970s, our enterprises continued to grow. Our enterprises proved they were strong enough to survive political issues. Had these events occurred in the '60s, the outcome would have been completely different. Even though Taiwan was still under an authoritarian political regime, our enterprises in the '70s were basically sound.

For a period of 20 years in the '60s and '70s when the country was undergoing industrialization, our society was evolving as well, but the political regime was stuck in the agrarian age. Other Little Dragons of Asia (ASIA NIES countries) followed similar patterns of development. Thus the establishment of a civilization begins with changes in the wealth-creating system,

then the social system changes and eventually changes engulf political system. Countries such as the Philippines, India and the USSR tried to by-pass this model by initiating change first in the political system but they all failed. Mainland China was relatively more successful because that they kept their political system intact. Under their authoritarian regime, Mainland China has initiated a series of changes in the wealth-creating and social system. From the perspective of Taiwan, the political system requires a long time to evolve. For the entire period of the 20 years of industrialization, no one on the island dared to talk openly about such political issues as elections.

Chapter **4**

Full Industrialization——Taiwan is Drowning in Money!

With money, you might not be happy; but without it, you'll definitely be blue.

——Anonymous

9.The 1980s

Changes in the Wealth-Creating System in the Period of Full Industrialization

I define the 1980s as a period of full industrialization. Taiwan passed out of the '60s when our economy was dependent on labor. We started setting up our own enterprises in the '70s. Then the enterprises grew significantly in the 1980s. Wages in the '60s were US$2-3, in the '70s US$10 and in the '80s US$100. In the '80s, per capita national income was US$2,300, our export value rose from US$2 billion to US$20 billion, and we had US$5.3 billion in foreign exchange reserves.

Monthly wage: US$100
Per capita national income: US$2,300
Export value: US$20 billion
Foreign exchange reserves: US$5.3 billion (1980)
          US$66 billion (1987)
          US$74 billion (1989)

1. Formation of Capital and Large-scale Enterprises

The textile and electronics industries were the primary engines of Taiwan's economy, and were further developed. The scope of their international operation was expanded. The plastics industry led by Wang Yung-ching and the steel industry by Chao Yao-tung （趙耀東） were among world leaders in their fields. The production volume of some 10 items produced in Taiwan including tennis rackets, bicycles and wicker chairs were ranked number one in the world.

2. The Rise of the Information Industry
The representative industry of the 1970s was the calculator industry whereas that of the '80s was the information industry. Let us take a look at how the information industry got its start.

a. The Suppression of Electronic Games
The information industry started off by making electronic games for kids. Even Acer began their operations by supplying ICs to electronic game makers. In the early 1980s, Lin Yang-kang （林洋港）, the Minister of the Interior, clamped down on the supply of electronic games. This move brought many companies which had depended on making electronic games fpr

Taiwan Experience

their livelyhood to the verge of bankruptcy. Once the products were disallowed, these companies could do nothing but switch to another product line i.e. the clome of Apple II products.

b. The Clome of Apple II products
Apple II was originally designed by some young engineers but their products were not well protected. It was very easy to copy these products and many Taiwanese manufacturers did in fact do so. But they were soon charged by Apple Inc. for copyright infringement. Local production lines therefore shifted to IBM-compatible personal computers.

Note: Apple II was the first 8-digit personal computer developed by Apple Inc. in the early '80s.

c. IBM-Compatible Personal Computers
The IBM-compatible PC was first launched on the market in 1981. Due to its open architecture, the IBM-compatible PC was soon adopted as the standard for the industry. Some Taiwanese companies pooled their experience and wealth and began to produce IBM-compatible PCs.

We have to give credit to two important persons who helped make the compatible PC industry a successful one in Taiwan. One is Li Kuo-ting, a high-ranking government official who fully supported and assisted the development of the industry. The other one is Stan Shih who represented the private sector. Thanks to their persistent efforts they helped create the IBM-compatible PC industry in Taiwan.

d. Two-Bay Strategy (made in Taiwan and sold by San Francisco Chinese)
How did we manage to sell computers? Taiwan used to made cheap items worth only a few US$ dollars a piece. How did Taiwan end up selling computers whose unit price was around US$1,000? Well, people in the industry figured out a "two-bay strategy" i.e. making computers in Taiwan and having San Francisco Chinese sell them. Near San Francisco is Silicon Valley. Many overseas Chinese were employed there during the day and sold Taiwan-made computers after working hours. Americans found out that these Chinese were skilled in sales, expertise and maintenance. Some Chinese ended up earning more during off-hours than they did from their full-time jobs.

They therefore quit their jobs and started their own companies selling computers. That was how we started selling Taiwan-made computers.

Note: The second syllable of Tai-wan (i.e. wan) carries the meaning of bay. The two bays in English refers to Tai-wan and San Francisco Bay

f. Self-owned Brand Names and "Small-Villages-Encompass-Big-Cities" Strategy

In 1984 Stan Shih proposed a concept advocating self-owned brand names. As computer production accounted for only 1% of total production, Taiwan-made computers were not attractive enough on the international market. We had to go outside Taiwan to promote and to sell. The "two-bay strategy" was like a hit-and-run battle and sales could have been better. Why didn't we establish our own brand names and sell them through joint efforts? We tried to do so but failed in the big USA market. Well, then we took a "small-villages-encompass-big-cities" strategy, i.e. we began selling first to smaller countries. The strategy was to establish an agency relationship with companies in smaller countries and thereby gradually penetrate into the markets of bigger countries. This was an important marketing strategy that helped Acer take off. Another strategy was to use components and peripherals as a way to eventually sell finished products.

f. Components and Peripherals Lead to Finished Products

It made sense to say that the Americans would not buy computers from Taiwan since the USA itself was a computer kingdom. However, we could and did sell them computer peripherals and components. We provided peripherals such as keyboards, mother boards, monitors, computer cases, PC boards, mice, power supplies and so on. After a while, Americans found out that the components and peripherals of their computers were all made in Taiwan. This was how we started selling computers via peripherals and components.

The information industry in the early 1980s brought a very hard time that lasted until 1988 when Acer and a few other computer companies were first listed on the stock market. By then the scale of their operations

had increased significantly.

3. Sharp Appreciation of NT$ in years 1986-1989 (from 40:1 to 26:1)

The sharp appreciation of the NT dollar against the US dollar in the '80s proved to be a disaster for many exporters. The exchange rate was originally set at 40:1 but rapidly changed to 26:1 in a period of three years.Thus, an exporter could originally convert his export value of US$1 million into a value of NT$40 million, but after appreciation, he could only get NT$26 million at the new exchange rate. It was like a death penalty for many exporters. An exporter might probably earn a profit of NT$5 million if he received an exchanged value at the rate of NT$40 million. Now that he only got NT$26 million, his company was in the red. Theoretically, this was a critical situation for many export-oriented enterprises. On the other hand, the monetary strategy worked as a challenge to test the adaptability of Taiwanese enterprises.

Let us take a look at some interesting figures. Our foreign exchange reserves in 1980 were up to US$5.3 billion. The figure was increased to US$66 billion in 1987 and US$74 billion in 1989. Where did the money come from? How could we accumulate such a huge amount of foreign exchange reserves in such a short period?

Taiwanese export-oriented enterprises used to save their foreign currencies abroad since they had no confidence in Taiwanese politics. Therefore, in the years between 1970 and 1985, our government superficially did not own significant foreign exchange reserves but nevertheless our exporters had made savings of billions of US$ abroad. With the sharp appreciation of the NT$, exporters remitted their foreign currencies back to Taiwan. That is one of the reasons why Taiwan suddenly became the richest country in the world. It was not possible to earn such a huge amount of foreign exchange reserves in such a short period. The amount was remitted from abroad during the said period. However, the excess foreign exchange reserves resulted in an excess of NT dollars that in turn brought about a surge in money games.

4. The Loss of GSP

Another unfortunate issue happened in 1987 when we were deprived of the GSP (Generalized System of

Preferences). With the GSP, we enjoyed waiving tariff duties for products exported to the US. The tariffs ranged from 3- 5% depending on the product line. With the loss of the 3-5% deduction on import taxes, many exporters could no longer make significant profits.

5. Enterprises' Outbound Expansion

In response to the sharp appreciation of the NT$ and the cancellation of the GSP, many Taiwanese companies were forced to move to Southeast Asia and Mainland China in the late '80s for survival, in spite of the government's opposition. This proved that in the late '80s our economy was a full industrialized one. Our enterprises were now capable of exporting capital and expertise.

Let us see what happened to the social system following the change occurred in the wealth-creating system.

10.Social Waves of the 1980s

The Societal Changes Accompanying the Full Industrialization

1. NT$100,000 per Household Ping (3.305 m2 or 35.58 ft.2)

The price of real estate soared and some houses were sold at NT$100,000 per ping. Back then the most expensive dwelling was called Twin-Diamond Building, located on Tunhua South Road. I heard that President Chiang Ching-kuo once sent people to check the source of capital for this building.

2. Social Disruption

Taipei was turning into a decadent society. Social conduct degenerated with more and more people indulging themselves in wining, dining, merrymaking and night life.

3. Touring Abroad

It is probably difficult for people of today to imagine how difficult it was to conduct overseas sightseeing tours which were liberalized only in 1991. Since then even grandpa and grandma have managed to go

abroad for sightseeing. Overseas sightseeing tours cost us a great deal in terms of the loss of foreign currency but sightseeing gives us access to many new ideas and information from abroad.

4. Real-Estate Tycoons

At first the government planned to seize those who were selling real estate at NT$10,000 per household ping. However, it was not possible to put such a plan into action. It turned out that almost all households were being sold at the said price or even higher. The big local enterprises earned significant amounts of NT$ and became real-estate tycoons.

5. Money Games

Since 1986 our society has been swept by a wave of money games, which included the purchase of traditional illegal lottery tickets, casino-like gambling, investment in stocks and other speculation activities. Money games have became a popular pastime.

6. Sumptuous Living

It happened that a single steak entree could cost between NT$8,000 and NT$14,000 in a restaurant. In the United States a good steak might cost around US$10 - 20. In Taiwan the same steak cost US$500! You can imagine just how extravagant life had become.

7. Worsening Social Condition

Incidents of kidnapping and blackmail were constantly in the news during this period. The situation was improved only in 1990 when Hau Pao-tsung (郝柏村) was appointed Premier and he initiated stiff anti-crime measures.

8. Tsi-chi Charity Committee (慈濟功德會)

While the society was getting worse, the Tsi-chi Charity Committee brought into society a breath of fresh air. The Committee was established by a nun called Master Cheng Yen (證嚴上人). Once she had noticed a pool of blood on the floor of a private hospital. She asked what had happened and learned that a poor aboriginal woman who couldn't afford the cost of hospital treatment was sent away without any care. After the event, Cheng Yen made a vow to establish a hospital that would provide care for all in need. With her faith and loving heart, she was able to found the Tsi-chi Hospital with the support of many

followers. She had the power to motivate people to do good for their fellow human beings. By the late '80s, it was said that there was one Tsi-chi member for every six persons in Taiwan.

The Tsi-chi Charity Committee reminds me of a story. A little bird held a small stone in its beak and was trying to fill up a big pond in which many kids had drowned. Everyone laughed at its efforts. Since it could hold only a single small stone at a time, how long would it take to fill up such a big pond? The little bird answered, "I'll keep on trying!" and it continued. The bird's efforts moved God. The God therefore filled up the pond overnight. The story of Master Cheng Yen inspired us with the love that move even heaven. The prosperity of Chi-tsi Charity Committee had proved that many people in Taiwan have good hearts.

I've worked so hard, I'm no longer afraid of any future struggle.

Bravo!

Heaven will exhaust your physique and test your mental strength if He gives you a major task to bear. "

That's right!

11.Political Waves of the 1980s

Changes in the Political System During the Period of Full Industrialization

It happened to me in 1979. On my way to a meeting at the Industrial Development Bureau, I noticed a book entitled "Who is the Successor of Chiang Ching-kuo?" at a street-side book stand. I bought the book immediately and carefully hid it in my jacket. Then I looked around to make sure that nobody had noticed me. Back home, I showed this book to my friends and relatives. Taiwanese society was still under a coercive and authoritarian regime, and the author must have had a lot of guts to write such a book. Nowadays, the appearance of such a book would no longer raise any eyebrows.

1. Freedom of Speech and Anti-KMT Publications

At the beginning of the '80s, the most interesting pastime was to read anti-KMT literature. These were banned publications written by non-KMT persons who revealed the dark side of government politics. Despite strict governmental censorship, these books were sold at street-side book stands. The stand owner would first give you a wink and then lead you to a corner to show you all the anti-KMT magazines, current best sellers that were outperforming pornography at the time. These book vendors made great profits by selling anti-KMT publications. In the late 1980s, the ban was finally lifted.

2. Political Mitigation

In 1987 those who were involved in the famous 1979.12.10 Formosa Magazine Incident. (美麗島事件) were released from jail. These people included Huang Hsin-jei （黃信介）、Yao Chia-wen（姚嘉文）、Lin Yi-hsiung（林義雄）and others. Then the Martial Law and bans on establishing new newspapers and political parties had all been lifted. The Democratic Progressive Party (DPP) was officially registered as a legal party in1989. (The DPP was established on Sept. 28, 1986)

Note: "Formosa" was the title of a magazine published by a group of non-KMT members. They expressed their views critical of the government and reported the little known dark side of the political leaders of the time. They advocated the lifting of the ban on

Taiwan Experience

establishing newspapers and political parties. The magazine included extensive reports criticizing the bias and errors of the government. The magazine advocated freedom of speech, the right to assembly, and the reshuffling of the National Assembly.

3. Liberalization of Family Visits to Mainland China

Taiwanese residents have been allowed to visit their family members in mainland China since Nov. 1, 1987. This enlightened policy was introduced by Chiang Ching-kuo before his passing. Contacts between the two sides of the Taiwan Strait were established. Though I did not have any relatives in the mainland, I went there to get a better grasp of the situation there.

4. The Passing of Chiang Ching-kuo

President Chiang Ching-kuo passed away in Jan. 1988. His selfless dedication and sacrifice throughout his lifetime for the welfare of the Taiwanese people assures him of an honored place in Chinese history.

5. Tienanman Event

On June 4 of 1989, the tragic event of Tienanmen erupted in Beijing. From one aspect, the event challenged communist control. On the other hand, it was also a blessing for the Chinese communists. Since then senior communists have began to pay attention to the opinions of Chinese youth. The young communists no longer concentrated entirely on political affairs, instead, they have switched some of their attention to the economy.

6. Parliamentary Fighting and the Collapse of Public Power

Since the end of the 1980s, the parliament became a stage for fist-fighting shows. It seems that people have lost their respect for the justice and public power.

The '80s was an agitating age. Let us see what happened to the way people think.

This issue of FORMOSA reveals why General Wang Sheng resigned. The contents are marvelous.

12. Waves of Thought of the 1980s

Changes in the Way of Thinking in the Period of Full Industrialization

The political system and the way people think in the '60s and the '70s are described together in this section. Back then people were afraid to think too much, hence the political system and people's thought were well integrated. Since the lifting of Martial Law in 1987, people began to be more free and independent in their thinking. Differences first appeared between the north and the south of Taiwan.

1. An Age of Confusion (the gap between the north and the south)

Northern Taiwan was industrialized whereas the central and southern Taiwan was still based on agricultural life. Therefore, a gap in thinking between the people in the north and the south came about.

2. Challenges to Traditional Values

Money games changed people's values. I had a friend who used to phone me for borrowing NT$100,000 or 200,000. To the best of my knowledge, he used the money to invest in the stock market. One day he phoned me to ask for advice. I thought that he wanted to borrow money from me once again. This was not the case. He drove his Benz to pick me up. He told he had earned about 10 or 20 million in the stock market. He wanted to invite me for a nice meal to show his appreciation for my support in the past. About half a year later, he phoned me again and said, "Dear Wen, I have capital of 96 million. I would have 100 million if I had another 4 million. Could you help if I want to invest in your company?" I replied, " My company is in good shape and so far we have no plan to raise capital." After the conversation I did not hear from him again for about one year. One day I went with my kid to play some electronic games in a store. I saw a man wearing a worn-out jacket. I took a closer look and noticed that the man was my friend Lee. Why in the world would he play games here? Where was his 96 million? All he had was gone. He turned out to be poorer than before.

Of course this was an individual case. But there have been many similar stories that have challenged our traditional values.

In the '80s our wealth-creating system became fully industrialized. Many changes occurred in our society. Our political system became more open and our ways of thinking system were also changing.

The 30 years from the '60s to the '90s represent an epoch of industrialization for Taiwan. Before we form a clearer picture of industrialization, Taiwan was developing a new civilization. Let us take a look at the figures from the '90s:

Monthly wage: US$800
Per capita national income: US$8,000
Export value: US$80 billion
Foreign exchange reserves: US$80 billion

The Period of Full Industrialization in the '80s .
Thanks to the depreciation of the US dollar, The average monthly wage amounted to US$800 which I personally felt was not too high. Per capita national

income reached US$8,000 and the export value rose from US$20 billion to US$80 billion. Our foreign exchange reserves increased from US$5.3 billion to US$80 billion. These were the famous four-8 figures for that time.

During this period Taiwan encountered a significant change. We entered a new epoch of wealth-creating system, that is, a system that creates wealth by knowledge.

Taiwan Experience

I showed off quite well by having a steak that cost NT$15,000.

That amount of NT$15,000 is not much. I spent 250,000 on my lunch.

What did you eat for such a large sum?

I had two fish.

Incredibe!

Chapter **5**

New Wealth-Creating System ——Creating a Wealth Through Knowledge

The fool seeks happiness from afar while the wise plants happiness under his feet.

——James Oppenheim

13. The 1990s

Knowledge Makes Money - the New Age of the Third-Wave Civilization

The first-wave of agrarian civilization created wealth by land and landlords possessed the dominant power. The second-wave of industrial civilization created wealth by capital and the rich had the dominant power. The third-wave of civilization however creates wealth by knowledge. Some Taiwanese enterprises since 1990 were leaning toward this direction. But at the same time we encountered "the black hole of China."

1. The Black Hole of China
In 1976 Mao Tse-tung passed away. Teng Hsiao-ping became the national leader in 1977. A series of revolutions and liberalizations took place in the '80s. In the '90s the events on Tienanmen occurred. Since that time, many outstanding youths in China began to focus their attention and energy to economic issues instead of political ones. Over the course of seven years, China absorbed from abroad capital of more than US$180 billion, which gives China foreign exchange reserves that exceed those of Taiwan. In

addition to these huge capital, many Chinese from Hong Kong and Taiwan have set up factories in China, bringing to China much-needed technology and management know-how. Furthermore, China is attractive due to her people's hard-working attitude and quick learning capability. In the 1990s China became like a black hole that sucked up the industrial infrastructure and achievements made by the accumulated efforts of Taiwanese people over thirty years. We have gone through the decades of the '60s, '70s and the '80s and emerged world leaders in manufacturing such products as umbrellas, Christmas lamps, bicycles, clothing, shoes, etc. However, these industries have also been sucked up by the black hole of China.

2. Keep the Roots

In the '90s, the black hole of China absorbed Taiwan's experiences that had been accumulated over the past 30 years, including its capital and skills. Concerned about this phenomenon, our government advocated the policy that enterprises keep their roots in Taiwan. I don't exactly understand what it means to keep one's roots in Taiwan. When Wang Yung-ching decided to

The Black Hole of China

invest in Hai-Tsung (海滄), Hsia-Men (廈門), our government advised him to keep his roots in Taiwan. Wang Yung-ching then replied, "What if I remit the earned profits back to Taiwan? Does this move account for keeping my roots in Taiwan?"

As I delved deeper in analyzing the issue, I found out that the entrepreneurs and the politicians are different in nature. For example, a politician representing the Chungshan district of Taipei has to be very familiar with the people and the customs of his district. He is like a tree planted in a specific area. An entrepreneur however has to survive by competition. He is like an animal running to and fro in a forest. Due to his different nature, the animal-like entrepreneurs have problems understanding why the tree-like politicians always declare the need to "keep your roots." Let me cite another example. If a candidate for the legislature of the Shihlin district is supported by the people in his district, he might be successfully elected. However, an entrepreneur, though he may be supported by all the residents of the Shihlin district, he can not survive without orders. That is why the slogan of keeping one's roots was so conflicting for entrepreneurs.

According to the interpretations of some officials, to keep one's roots is to maintain R&D (research & development) in Taiwan while moving out production units. It sounds reasonable at first glance. However, entrepreneurs have their specific competitive advantages: some are strong in marketing, some in R&D and some in production. Most Taiwanese entrepreneurs have a competitive edge in production. What is the use to keep the relatively weak R&D in Taiwan? And what about problems of integration problem if we do separate the R&D from production? Neither is a reason for keeping one's roots.

Therefore, no matter how risky it is, the black hole of China continues absorbing investments from Taiwan. For many Taiwanese enterprises, China is the best choice for investment, with the same language and similar management styles and systems. It is difficult to attract investment in the Caribbean. How can Taiwanese enterprises operate their businesses in a strange, far-away and sophisticated market? In this situation, Taiwan's traditional industries have kept moving to China and, as a result, we discover new opportunities for Taiwan.

Taiwan Experience

3. Taiwan's New Opportunities (capital-intensive, technology-intensive, speed-intensive)

Taiwanese enterprises strong in the following aspects have a potential for success.

a. Capital-intensive

Even though the amount of Taiwan's foreign exchange reserves no longer ranks first in the world, the per capita foreign exchange reserves far exceeds that of any other country. This means that Taiwan enjoys an affluence of capital existing mostly in cash. In the past, investment in Taiwan focused on processing industries that did not require huge capital outlays.

b. Technology-intensive

The calculator industry in the '70s and the computer and the IC industry in the '80s required many trained engineers. In addition, a huge brain gain from the US took place. Thus, Taiwan can boast of a large number of skilled experts.

c. Speed-intensive

Taiwan is relatively lax in regard to enforcing rules and

regulations. We see cars speeding down all the main streets and without any regard for law. According to western standards, this situation would be intolerable. However, here we reach our destination at a quicker speed. This is our advantage. Taiwan's opportunities lie on the industries intensive in capital, technology and speed.

4. Taiwan's New Industries (capital-, technology- and speed-intensive)

The black hole of China has absorbed many of the traditional industries of Taiwan. But at the same time, Taiwan discovers new opportunities in new industries.

a. IC Industry (OEM IC fundry and memory IC)

The IC industry was seeded in the '70s and planted in the '80s. During the ten years of its development, IC industry was fueled by the fever of money games. It absorbed a huge sum of capital from the stock market. As we know, the IC industry is a capital- and technology-intensive industry. In the early stage of its development, Taiwan's IC industry mainly consisted of OEM IC fundry orders and memory chips.

In the late '80s, our IC companies grew rapidly - much

faster than any other IC companies in the world. Our profits on returns were also much higher than those of our foreign competitors. The main reason is that we are quicker. Taiwanese stay up overnight to innovate products and to follow up on orders. Our speed is incredible. Therefore, the IC industry became the main industry of our country. In 1995 we had a trade surplus of US$8.1 billion, among which US$2 billion was materialized by the five leading IC companies in Taiwan.

b. PCs, Mother Boards and Computer Peripherals
The PC industry headed by Acer started budding in the early '80s. The industry grew significantly in the late '80s. Since 1995, it has been the largest exporting industry of Taiwan. It is also a representative Taiwanese industry - intensive in capital, technology and speed.

C. Notebook Computer
The notebook industry followed as a brilliant star. This popular industry is based on information technologies developed in the past. It also has the advantage of the calculator - it is thin, light, short and small. The

notebook industry has provided Taiwan with great opportunities. In 1996 the export value of notebooks amounted to US$6 billion, ranking first in Taiwan in terms of unit export items. The notebook is also the most expensive electronic product in terms of unit price. Today the unit price for a notebook is US$4,000. It means that the cost of two notebooks is equivalent to a passenger car. There is no doubt that the industry has significant importance and potential.

The above-mentioned three industries are obvious examples. In the future Taiwan will certainly develop more industries that are intensive in capital, technology and speed.

Let us look at what happened to our society under the new wealth-creating system that centered on knowledge-derived wealth.

14. The Social Waves of the 1990s

Social Changes Along With a New Wealth-Creating System

1. Housing at Sky-high Price

In the '70s the price for one household ping was NT$10,000, in the '80s it was NT$100,000, in the '90s the price skyrocketed. A house of NT$400,000 or NT$500,000 per ping was nothing special. The sky-high price had two meaning: it was too expensive and it reached its peak. In Tokyo, real-estate prices fell down 40% after reaching their peak. Sooner or later prices in Taiwan will fall. We can imagine the decreasing power of the real-estate tycoons.

2. The Fourth TV Station (Cable TV)

The fourth TV station created new challenges for the police and system operators. In its early phase, cable TV was illegal. The police would cut cable lines in the morning and within a few minutes the cable was reconnected by cable TV providers. Since there was no laws nor relevant regulations governing cable TV, how did the fourth TV station arise? As the wealth-creating system changed, people made money by their knowledge. The public therefore was in need of more knowledge and information. They could no longer be satisfied with the existing three wireless TV channels. Therefore, the fourth station offered multiple channels came into being and prospered. This is the phenomenon that often occurs in an information society. During the early stages of development, cable TV programs were copied without authorization as the channels were all illegal. The development of cable TV took place so fast that even Japan and the US fell behind us. Our government therefore could do nothing but legalize cable TV operations. Today, the availability of cable TV in Taiwan is probably number one or two in the world.

3. KTV Culture

Other changes also took place in our society. One popular activity in the '80s was to listen to singers singing in night clubs. In the '90s, KTV (karaoke TV) became very popular. People gathered in a room to dine, drink, sing and dance. This is a typical phenomenon in an information society. In industrialized societies, an entertainment program in a club is arranged by someone else while in an information society you arrange your own program. You pay the rent for a room and then arrange everything yourself. This pastime indicates that our society is approaching toward an information society. KTV is actually a substitute for MTV (Movie TV). People used to watch small-screen movies in a private room. Then MTV owners were caught by the police because of the unauthorized screenings of foreign movies. Suddenly, all MTV owners changed their businesses to run KTVs. Taiwanese specialize in finding new opportunities from lostones. When the police clamped down on electronic games, owners survived by changing their product line to computers. When charged with operating unauthorized MTVs, they changed their

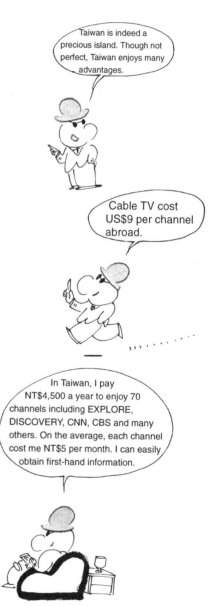

Taiwan is indeed a precious island. Though not perfect, Taiwan enjoys many advantages.

Cable TV cost US$9 per channel abroad.

In Taiwan, I pay NT$4,500 a year to enjoy 70 channels including EXPLORE, DISCOVERY, CNN, CBS and many others. On the average, each channel cost me NT$5 per month. I can easily obtain first-hand information.

business line to KTVs.

4. Human Assets

In a traditional financial report, human factors were regarded as deficits while desks and chairs were assets. However, in an information society, wealth is made by knowledge and therefore humans are assets. When Taiwan's private banks were first established, they offered an annual salary of NT$100 million in trying to recruit general managers or presidents from public banks. It showed that our society valued human assets. During the period when stock prices were soaring, the profits a brokerage firm earned were much more than those earned by Nan Ya Plastics, the largest private corporation of Taiwan. Money games were like an impetus that makes people value human assets and information. Indeed, in a wealth-creating system in which money comes with knowledge, human assets and information are of vital importance.

5. Politician Fever

Many people have said that Taiwan has high fever for politics. I don't think so. It is a fever for politicians. Most people have no clear idea about the nature of

politics. In fact, most people just listen to what a politician speaks about. Tomorrow we follow another politician who talks about something else. People just follow the media. This is a special social phenomenon in the 1990s.

Let us look at the political changes accompanying the new wealth-creating and social systems in the '90s.

15. The Political Waves of the 1990s

Political Changes Along With the New Wealth-Creating System

1. February Political War
In one February of the early '90s, Lee Teng-hui and Lin Yang-kung fought for national leadership. At the end they shook hands to symbolize national harmony. This initiated the age of Lee Tung-hui.

2. The Age of Lee Tung-hui
With personal perseverance and cultivation, Lee Tung-hui has been persistent in bringing about an American-style democracy in Taiwan. Burdened with thousands years of Chinese history and the regime of the two Chiangs, the Taiwanese regard the political leader as a governor as well as a focus of faith. The people are used to a "strong-man" style of leadership. This has helped Lee Tung-hui to become a "strong-man" powerful leader and to create his age.

3. Seeking an American-style Democracy
History has proved that only two political systems can peacefully transfer political power in an industrialized

society. One is American-style democracy, the other is the British-style. They are also called the presidential system and the cabinet system, respectively. I think that the difference between the two systems is not as simple as that between the President and the cabinet. They are two different democratic systems. We know that political control is authoritarian in an agrarian socity. As long as we paid taxes and remain docile, we don't mind being controlled. Under the different wealth-creating system of an industrialized society, people live more closely to one another. It is not proper to continue the authoritarian political system of an agrarian society. Things that seemed none of our business turned out to be our business. That is why in many countries political revolutions follow industrial revolutions. In Great Britain there was a Constitutional Kingdom, in France a Grand Revolution, and in the USA the Civil War. According to Toffler's explanation, the political system of an agrarian society is transformed into a new one for the industrialized society. This is the conflict between two types of politics. Taiwan's political system in the agrarian period could only be maintained until the '80s . In the late '80s the Democratic Progressive Party was established and the authoritarian system collapsed. Since then Taiwan has been following the American-type democracy.

4. Media Politics

The American-type democracy gives rise to media politics. Many people would agree that American presidential elections depend heavily on the media and therefore give rise to media politics. Currently, Taiwan has become the country that has the most extensive media coverage of politics in the world.

5. National Campaign for Election

Political elections have become a national campaign. The voting rate in Japan and the US is lower than 50% but in Taiwan it is higher than 80%.

These are the changes in the political environment under the new wealth-creating system of the '90s. Let us continue to see what changes have occurred in the way people think.

16.Waves of Thought in the 1990s

Changes in Thinking Under the New Wealth-Creating System

1. Social Adaptability Syndrome (agrarian, industrial and information people live together)
The social adaptability syndrome hit home. A period of 50 years is short, people of the agrarian age in the '60s, those of the industrial age in '60s-'90s and those of the information age since 1990 are all alive and we live together in the same society. Our society is therefore a composite of agrarian, industrial and information civilizations. If we turn on cable TV and quickly review all available programs, we realize that there are programs specifically target the agricultural people, some are for the industrial people and some for the information people.

2. The Trend Towards Polarity (network group and back-to-the-past group)
The society is polarized. People in the '90s are even further divided into two extremes; one is the network group and the other is the back-to-the-past group.

a. The Network Group

A networking device is more than a new technology. It carries significant meaning by changing people's way of obtaining information from "on receipt" to "on demand". Before the internet was available, people used to get information or messages on receipt. In this way, we would receive information provided by someone else. For example, every morning we receive newspapers delivered to the door of our house. We would turn on television to watch provided programs and we would read books and magazines sent to us. We find books displayed in a library or find goods from show rooms. This is a passive way of getting information. The internet stores all kinds information on the hard disk of a computer. Information in different computers is connected by a network system. In this way information is obtained "on demand". It means that we get whatever we want by means of a network system. For example, if we want to buy something, we can key in its specifications to a computer which will then search for me. This is an initiative way to get information. I think that internet is still a primitive technology. I believe that more devices for two-way communications will emerge in the near

future. We can get easy access to information "on receipt" and "on demand". The new generation is that of the network people. As long as you follow them and enter into the information society, you are an information person.

b. Back-to-the-past Group
There is another group of people who are accustomed to agrarian or industrial life. They refuse to change or they are very afraid of computers. They however cannot stay in between the old age and the new age. In fact, standing in between makes people very nervous. Therefore, these people choose to go back to the old days. That's why in Taiwan there are many liars who can fool the public and earn billions by donming religious attire. They are supported by the back-to-the-past group. This is the result of the polarized development in our social system and way of thinking.

17.Looking Back on the Past 50 years

The Search for Taiwan's Life Engine and the Creation of an Ever New Future

We have reviewed the wealth-creating system, the social system, the political system and the way of thinking of the agrarian age in the '50s. We have also seen that many changes occurred in the wealth-creating system, as well as in the social and political systems and the thinking of people of the industrial age between the '60s and the '90s. In two more years, human history will enter a new epoch with the year 2000. Looking back at the development of the past five decades, we find that there are many issues worth examining. We are very glad to see that although at the beginning we were not able to earn even one penny in wages, now the monthly wage in Taiwan is over US$1,000. The per capita national income started from US$80 but now the figure is over US$10,000. Our exports were originally very limited with a total export value of US$100 million, but now the figure is over US$100 billion. Our foreign exchange reserves have grown from zero to near US$100 billion

Taiwan Experience

at present. In fact, over the years, the total amount that Taiwanese enterprises invest or save abroad far exceeds the amount of foreign exchange reserves we have in Taiwan.

1. Negative Impacts

Have the developments over the past fifty years had any negative impact on us? Yes, they have. According to the analysis of professor Charles Kao (高希均), the following are the four most significant negative factors affecting the quality of life in Taiwan:

a. Environmental Deterioration

There is garbage everywhere and hundreds of thousands of stray dogs wandering the streets. You might wonder as I do why people feel free and comfortable to park their cars randomly on roadsides? Why do people freely park their motorcycles on public walkways? Why are people allowed to run their restaurant businesses and cook on public walkways? It is incredible to see such phenomena in Taiwan when we are proud of our economic power and development.

b. High Social Cost

No regulations governed KTV operations until after many people burned to death in KTV fires. We pay too much social cost in order to get attention on public safety issues.

c. Privilege and Monopoly

A household ping which cost NT$50,000 is sold at NT$300,000. Most people have to save money all their lives in order to afford an ordinary apartment. This phenomenon is due to the fact that a few people own most of the land in our society. Last year, I watched a TV program which reported that even in Calcutta, one of the poorest cities in the world, there is a subway available for the public. We have spent about US$18 billion in building the most expensive subway in the world, one which has been taking a long time to complete. These are the negative impacts upon land and public construction caused by improper privilege and monopoly.

d. Social Disorder and Invalid Laws

The laws and regulations have not been well enforced. On top of that, parliament has become an arena for fist-fighting, which has made situation even worse.

2. The Invisible Power

Should any newly rising country want to learn from the Taiwan experience and at the same time avoid the above-mentioned pitfalls, it would be very successful. On the other hand, I

personally think that people can always learn something positive from the negative. For example, even though the overall environment is deteriorating, many people in Taiwan still work hard to contribute to society. Many public officials, though not well paid, are willing to work overtime to get things done. Perhaps there is some invisible power that inspires people to do good. We can still say that the good people outnumber the bad ones. We often criticize our educational system but many talented people emerge from our schools. That is why I frequently mention that in Taiwan we have an invisible power.

I remember a story about two fighting birds. A man saw two birds fighting with each other. The owner of the winning bird was awarded a large sum of money. His friend encouraged him to invest in fighting birds. Therefore, he bought 100 fighting birds and locked them all in one cage. The next morning, he found out to his surprise that there was only one bird left in the cage. The other birds had all been killed. He immediately phoned his friend. His friend was very surprised to know that he was so stupid to put all his fighting birds in one cage. These birds are born with a fighting nature and they will of course fight against one another until they are all killed. His friend therefore advised him to buy new bird. He said, "I still have one left. And this must be the most powerful one." The story reminded me of my fellow people. Though we suffer in a polluted environment, from improper monopolies and privileges, and social disorder, we somehow still survive and in fact we go on living well. There must be an invisible power. Therefore, I am very confident of Taiwan's future

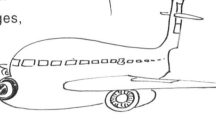

Grandma has never been abroad in all her life. This is the very first time she has boarded a plane. She wants to see if Hong Kong is really like a brilliant pearl and if America is really a merry country.

As we continue to develop, what will happen to us in the twenty-first century?

Here I will make some predictions in changes in the wealth-creating system. Predictions of changes in other systems will follow accordingly.

Taiwan Experience

Chapter **6**

Future Days——Let Ideals Bloom in Year 2000

The meaning of a man's being is not in what he gets but in what he aspires.

——Geblam

Cheer up! Let our ideals continue to shine in year 2000!

18.Creating a New Future

Forecast of Trends in 2000 - The Age of Electronic Information

1. A Single-industry Country (The information-related industry accounts for more the 50% of total exports)
Whether we like it or not, Taiwan will become a single-industry country by the year 2000. Currently the electronic information industry accounts for 25% of our total exports. If this trend continues, the information industry and its related industries will account for 50% of our total exports, making our country a single-industry one. It is like Switzerland whose watch industry accounts for almost 50% of the country's total exports. It does not mean that there is only one manufacturing activity in a single-industry country. It means that the total output of the single industry will account for more than 50% of the country's total exports. As our information industry continues its development, it will become the center of our IC industry and the precision machine-processing industry as well. Our communication industry will be based on

PC communication. There are also other industries that will develop in accordance with the information industry and eventually become information-related industries. The overall amount will account for 50% of our total exports and make Taiwan a single-industry country.

As a result, electronic tycoons will appear.

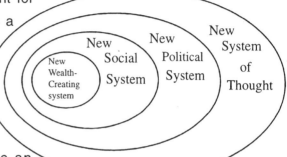

2. Electronic Tycoons-- Products for Exports
Today many electronic companies have an income of NT$5 billion or 10 billion. It is not difficult to predict that in the near future these export-oriented electronic billionaires will replace real-estate billionaires. These well-educated and high-tech-minded billionaires will certainly make an impact upon our society and politics.

3. Media Giants -- Products for the Domestic Market
Media giants will arise from the domestic market. As the internet provides mutual communication by an "on demand" system, we can deal with banks, insurance companies and department stores directly through internet. The internet will therefore replace many

traditional industries. At the same time, media giants will appear on cable TV. During the presidential election last year, some TV stations earned billions of NT$ in advertising fees in just one month by broadcasting a TV debate. We can see that the media, including KTV, are in the mainstream of domestic sales. We can envision that the media giants will cover the major domestic markets in the near future.

4. The Vanguard of Information Civilization

New wealth-creating system–wealth is created by information.

Last but not least, we believe that Taiwan, after the year 2000, will soon build up an information civilization in which wealth is created by information. We will be among a handful of countries that will advance into an information civilization. We will establish a new wealth-creating system, and therefore a new social and political system, and new ways of thinking.

By making advantage of our intelligence, skills, knowledge and innovative ideas, we can certainly creat great wealth.

Chapter **7**

Give Thanks to Everyone

If we do not see heaven, we shall have to create one.

——Anonymous.

 Taiwan Experience

Special thanks to Adviser Li Kuo-ting for his counsel and preface. Thanks to President Wu Jung-yi of the Taiwan Economic Research Institute for his encouragement and preface. Also thanks to Yeh Tsi-hua (葉紫華, wife of Stan Shih) and Chung Chin-chu (張青駒), former President of Electronic Research & Service Organization) for the corrections they made of the writing in this book. Many thanks to those who worked behind the scenes. Let us also give thanks to the Taiwan Experience that made you and me what we are today.

A Cartoonist's Taiwan Experience

——Cartoon Diary of Tsai Chi-Chung

I was born in a small village called "Hwa Tan" (which means "Flower Pot") in central Taiwan. The village leans against a mountain.

"Flower Pot" village not true to her name, is not blessed with fields of beautiful flowers. There is neither gorgeous mountain view nor serene river valley setting; nevertheless, the village itself is quite pretty.

When we were little, we never said we were from Flower Pot village. Instead, we said we were from "Under-a-big-tree" village. "Under-a-big-tree" was the nickname of Flower Pot village. There was a big tree in Flower Pot village, hence the nickname. The tree was about 500 meters from where I live.

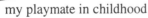

my playmate in childhood

My home village is called "under-a-big-tree" village.
I was the little boy who used to play under the big tree.

Profile of a little boy from "under-a-big-tree" village.

Birthday
Feb. 2, 1948

I had the bad habit of scratching my skin which always itched from mosquito and flea bites.

My head and hair smelt bad as I always wore medicated patches.

I was not fat at all. My bloated belly was caused by a roundworm living inside me.

My pants and underpants were made from a Sino-American Flour sack. There was no difference between the two as I only had one pair of pants.

Emptiness

I worked in mountainous area not too far from the sea.
Therefore, my feet were frequently scratched by tall weeds and looked like two red-bean poles.

I had a bamboo savings box with my name on it. The savings box, however, was always empty with not even a penny in it.

Spring, 1951

You could say that I grew up nourished by America. Soon after I was born, I was brought by my parents to baptized by an American priest in a church.

The church served as a window that opened up toward the western world . The window also provided me w access to western religion, philosophy, cartoons, west civilization and western goods including butter, milk, clothes, etc. Church life has had a profound influence upon my whole life.

At the age of two or three, I used to read lots of comic strips available in the church. Maybe that is why I became a cartoonist when I grew up.

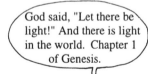

My predilection for philosophical thinking originates from the stories of the Old Testament and the New Testament taught in Bible study class.

Our church delivered US-aid material to church members every two months.

Butter, milk and corn powder from the USA probably made me more intelligent.

↓ (American Red Beans)

↑ (Corn Powder)

However, clothing form the USA gave me one big headache!

Mama! American insects are biting me!

Summer, 1952

My uncle was a fruit peddler. During the summer peak fruit season, he usually enjoyed a good cash flow. He was in fact the only source of my pocket

Dear uncle always passed by my house on his way to a merchandise store. I used to stop him and see if there was any penny hidden in his ears for me.

People from rural areas used to wear simple shirts and shorts without pocket. Ears therefore became the best place to put your coins.

Winter, 1952

People were poor when I was little. It was never possible to keep any money overnight. However, every kid owned a savings bank made by his or her papa.

rumbling

I am starving! How I long for a penny's worth caramel candies!

Take a look and see if there are any savings in the bamboo box.

A savings box made out of bamboo.

What? I don't hear anything..

I am starving, too. You never feed me with coins!

This was in fact very true...

A savings box that never had a penny in it overnight.

Summer, 1953

The Hwa electric floor fan was the first high-tech product owned by my family. It was also the most expensive commodity we had. It cost NT$900, equivalent to two months of my father's wages..

It swings to and fro!

Be careful not to break the fan. It cost your father NT$900 and he had to ask for a loan from the Farmers' Association.

What's a "loan"?

The breeze created by an NT$900 electrical fan is of course cooler than that by a 1NT$ fan.

Fall, 1953

The vegetables we ate in rural area were simple but were organic food. We planted the vegetables by ourselves. There was no residues of chemical fertilizers or pesticides.

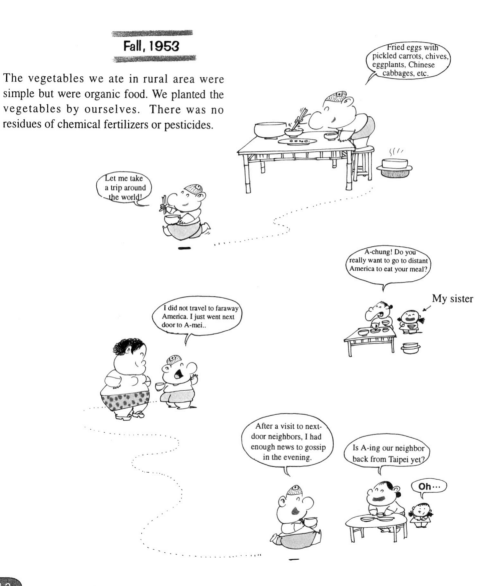

Fried eggs with pickled carrots, chives, eggplants, Chinese cabbages, etc.

Let me take a trip around the world!

A-chung! Do you really want to go to distant America to eat your meal?

My sister

I did not travel to faraway America. I just went next door to A-mei..

After a visit to next-door neighbors, I had enough news to gossip in the evening.

Is A-ing our neighbor back from Taipei yet?

Oh···

After graduating from primary school, most rural children left home to work in cities. They had to earn money to support their families. At that time, the most common job for a boy was a laborer in a cement factory, and for a girl a housemaid who did the cooking and laundry in big cities. A job in a textile plant was quite a decent one at that time for a female worker.

Taiwan Experience

I entered primary school at the age of six, one year earlier than other kids. My biggest dream was to have a well-equipped pencil box as I was convinced that doing a good job requires efficient instruments.

A colorful plastic pencil box with a two-color rubber eraser, a ruler 15 centimeters long, a pencil knife, some perfumed pencils and

I had been dreaming of getting one for a whole year until one day I happened to find a purse.

My dream came true!
A two-color rubber eraser cost 3 pennies, a knife 5 pennies, a yellow pencil with a rubber eraser 2 pennies, a pink perfumed pencil 5 pennies, a 15-cm ruler 5 pennies, a colorful plastic pencil box 1 dollar and 2 pennies. I still have 3 pennies to buy an icecream bar and some glass balls!

Wow! There are 15 dollars inside!

I get my reward!

Good !

Of course I did not give it to the police as I was taught by my school teachers. Instead, I gave it to my mom and got a reward of three and half dollars.

knife

two-color rubber eraser

yellow pencil

perfumed pencil

Say bye-bye to my wooden pencil box.

Fall, 1958

My family used to own a piece land that was 9,000m² for crops and 1 acre of land near the mountain. When my second eldest brother got married, my father offered him that 1 acre of mountain land so that he could be on his own.

Take this to support your own family and set up your business.

Good!

One acre of mountain land was worth about NT$28,000.

My brother sold out the land. The money he got was just enough to buy a motorcycle.

wow···

wow···

Oh···

A whole mountain could only be exchanged for a motorcycle. For the first time I realized how cheap agricultural civilization was! Industrial civilization was the one that could make you rich!

A 200 c.c. motorcycle   = NT$28,000
1 acre of mountain land = NT$28,000
A 200 c.c. motorcycle   = 1 acre of mountain land

135

Taiwan Experience

I came to Taipei on a local train leaving my village at 2:00 p.m. on July 25 in 1963. I was to start my cartoon career with 200NT$ given from my father and brother-in-law.

Summer, 1963

200NT$

Board plus 300NT$ a month. Is that acceptable?

Yes, I'll take it!

Guaranteed sweet pineapple. One slice for 5 pennies.

Delicious !

When I was new to Taipei, I missed the taste of my home-town pineapple more than anything. However I couldn't afford to pay 5 pennies a slice. To satisfy my longing, I bought one slice of pineapple core for one penny as a compromise.

Summer, 1965

In 1965 I began working for the largest comic strip publishing firm, Wen Chang Company. I was paid 6 dollars per page of comic strips. Normally there were 150 pages in a book and I was paid NT$900 per book. Every month I could finish one and a half books and had an income of NT$1,350.

(Western frontier)

Every time I handed over my cartoon works and got paid, I took a day off to shop for new clothing in the Shi-meng-ding area and went to a Hollywood movie.

I allow you to watch TV because you are nice to me.

I always remembered to bring some gifts for my boss' son. He was the one who let me watch TV.

Anyone who isn't nice to me is not allowed to watch TV in my living room!

COMBAT

Combat

Don't push!

"Combat" is good!

"The Desert Heros" is better.

I prefer "Traveling Around the World" and "Suspicions."

It's so hot here!

Taiwan Experience

Summer, 1968

On Sept. 24, 1968, two days before I entered the army, I went to a Korean movie that was about three orphans. I was deeply touched by this sad movie.

Well, eat three apples for dinner.

No.! I want rice. I don't want apples!

No!

No!

Even though the three kids were abandoned by their mother, at least each of them had three apples for dinner. I couldn't understand why they were crying as if were the end of the world.

Never in my life did I ever have a whole apple. Why don't these Korean children appreciate what they have?

A Taiwanese kid who grudged eating a whole apple by himself...

Taiwan withdrew from the United Nations in the third year of my military service. It was however not the biggest disaster for Taiwan. The biggest disaster was our Seven-Tiger little league baseball team losing to Puerto Rico in Williamsport.

Summer, 1970

Taiwan withdrew from the UN in 1971. The "Three Championships" won by our little league, teenage league and junior youth league baseball teams every year in the US became a national morale-booster for our people.

Fall, 1972

When I completed my military service, I started working in Kuang Chi Program Services Company. In the meantime, I began dating girls.

Young people at that time were all proud of their plan to study abroad in America. Male college students always talked their plans, whether they were true or not. Coeds would brag about their boy friends studying in the USA...

Fall, 1976

I worked for the Kuang Chi Program Service for 5 years.
My starting salary was NT$2,900 in 1971 then NT$5,400 in
1973, NT$9,200 in 1975 and NT$11,400 in 1976...

Taiwan Experience

Spring, 1977

The Dragon Cartoon Company

After the 1977 lunar new year, I established my own cartoon

The owners of newly founded businesses in Taipei were all around the age of 30. They belong to the post-war new generation that came from rural villages to make a living in Taipei. Communication and cooperation among one another were very easy as they were close in age and background.

Jan. 1984

After 7 years in operation, my cartoon company began profitable by making a series of cartoon commercial films and three movies including "The Old Man" and "Oug- Long House"

Everyone has been working very hard this year. I will give you an extra 1.5-month salary for the annual year-end bonus. Are you happy?

Not at all! The computer companies offer a 9-month salary for the year-end bonus!

Well! The cartoon is an industry as well as the computer one is. But the computer industry depends on automation whereas our cartoon industry depends on manual labor.

At the end of 1984, I realized that the computer industry would be the dominant industry of the future. The cartoon industry was a sunset industry that would soon be replaced by the computer industry. Therefore, I closed my cartoon company and began working on my own to make comic strips. Then I came out with works including "The Drunk Chivalry" and "Tsung Tsi".

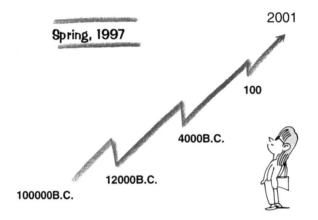

Spring, 1997

2001

100

4000B.C.

12000B.C.

100000B.C.

Human civilization has never advanced in a smooth and gradual steps.
It jumps and leaps in a series of eruptive and explosive steps.

Eight million years ago, mankind's ancestors started coming down from the trees. For a long period of space and time, there were only a few turning points that made human beings what we are today.

The control of fire

The invention of the wheel

The development of livestock and agriculture

ABCD

The development of language

The inventions and application of technologies

The accumulated knowledge and technology of eight million years fall far short of the technology and civilizations created by the people of the past several decades.

The globe is tending toward a brand new information age based on computers. No one can exclude remain outside the system. In a few years, we will enter the new epoch of the 21st century.

About every 30 years human beings witness a turning point that brings about a civilization lasting for a course of 1,000 years . Given the fact that human beings can live only a limited years on earth, we are very lucky to have been born in this information age which will span two millenia.

Let's work hard and take a chance to create our own future. The future of Taiwan and the world depends on how and what we do today.

What about ourselves? We belong to the generation that will determine our own future!

Hurrah!

A *smile* Book

Locus Publishing Company

Taipei County, Taiwan

2-3, Alley 20, Lane 142, Sec. 6, Roosevelt Road, Taipei, Taiwan

ISBN 957-8468-13-x Chinese Language Edition

ISBN 957-8468-38-5 English Language Edition

Copyright ©1997 by Sayling Wen &Tsai Chi-Chung

English Language Copyright © 1998 by Locus Publishing Company

All Rights Reserved

March 1998, First Edition

Printed in Taiwan

smile018

台灣經濟的苦難與成長

作者：溫世仁　繪圖：蔡志忠

英譯：吳良鈺　英譯審定：Joel Janicki

責任編輯：韓秀玫　封面設計：何萍萍

發行人：廖立文

出版者：大塊文化出版股份有限公司

台北市117羅斯福路六段142巷20弄2-3號

電話：(02)9357190　傳眞：(02)9356037

信箱：新店郵政16之28號信箱

讀者服務專線：080-006689

郵撥帳號：18955675　帳戶名：大塊文化出版股份有限公司

行政院新聞局局版北市業字第706號

總經銷：北城圖書有限公司　地址：台北縣三重市大智路139號

電話：(02)9818089(代表號)　傳眞：(02)9883028　9813049

製版印刷：源耕印刷事業有限公司

初版一刷：1998年3月　定價：新台幣180元

初版 3 刷：1999年 3 月

LOCUS

LOCUS